# Charly Antolini · Gerald Stütz

# Power Drums

## The Way I Play

Training, Tipps und Tricks
für fortgeschrittene Drummer
Training, Tips and Tricks
for advanced Drummers

ED 9279
ISMN M-001-12899-5

## SCHOTT

Mainz · London · Madrid · New York · Paris · Tokyo · Toronto
© 2000 Schott Musik International GmbH & Co. KG, Mainz · Printed in Germany

ED 9279
ISMN M-001-12899-5
ISBN 3-7957-5449-6

© 2000 Schott Musik International, Mainz
Umschlag und Gestaltung: H. J. Kropp
Printed in Germany · BSS 49 931

www.schott-music.com

# Inhalt

# Contents

# Die Autoren

## Charly Antolini

Am *24. 5. 1937* in Zürich geboren, bekam er schon in jungen Jahren an einer der berühmten Tambouren-Schulen seiner Heimatstadt die Grundausbildung als Trommler. Diese handwerkliche Ausbildung – schweizerisch-solide – prägte seine weitere musikalische Entwicklung entscheidend.

*1956* – mit neunzehn Jahren – startete er bereits in Paris seine Musikerlaufbahn als Profi und spielte alsbald mit so berühmten Jazz-Musikern wie Sidney Bechet, Albert Nicholas und Bill Coleman.

*1962* ging er nach Stuttgart. Unter anderem spielte er dort fünf Jahre im Südfunk-Tanzorchester unter Erwin Lehn. Engagements zu den Bigbands von Peter Herbolzheimer, Kurt Edelhagen, Max Greger und der Bigband des NDR schlossen sich an. In dieser Zeit entstanden zahlreiche Aufnahmen mit führenden Jazzmusikern des Swing und Bebop, wie beispielsweise Art van Damme, Roy Eldridge, Art Farmer, Buddy de Franco, Jimmy Giuffre, Dusko Goykovich, Earl Hines und Baden Powell.

*1979* machte Charly Antolini Furore mit der LP „Knock Out". Bereits wenige Tage nach ihrem Erscheinen war diese Platte bereits vergriffen. Die Musikstücke dieser LP zeigten Charlys explosiv-vitale Musikalität, sein überragendes Timing und die schweizerische Präzision seiner Schlagtechnik. Sie bestachen aber auch durch eine wahrhaft atemberaubende Dynamik, die seinerzeit so manchen mittelmäßigen Lautsprecher „Knock Out" gehen ließ.

*1981* holte ihn Benny Goodman, der „King of Swing", für eine Tournee in seine Band. Die Tournee führte durch Deutschland und Italien, und endete mit dem bereits legendären Konzert in Kopenhagen, das am 25. Dezember 1982 europaweit im Fernsehen ausgestrahlt wurde.

*1996* feierte Charly Antolini sein vierzigjähriges Jubiläum als professioneller Schlagzeuger.
Zu den Weggefährten dieser Jahre zählen: Bruce Adams, Benny Bailey, Sidney Bechet, Eugen Cicero, Wolfgang Dauner, Barbara Dennerlein, Silvia Droste, Herb Ellis, Booker Erwin, Bud Freeman, Joe Gallardo, Herb Geller, Fatty George, Jimmy Giuffre, George Gruntz, Steve Gut, Lionel Hampton, Earl Hines, Red Holloway, Peanuts Hucko, Helen Humes, Thad Jones, Oscar Klein, Brian Lemon, Albert Mangelsdorff, Butch Miles, Red Mitchell, Dick Morrissey, Danny Moss, Romano Mussolini, Sal Nistico, Nippy Noya, Nils-Henning Örsted-Pedersen, Rebecca Parris, Fritz Pauer,

# About The Authors

## Charly Antolini

Born on *24 May 1937* in Zurich, he received his basic education as a drummer at one of the famous drummer schools in his hometown at an early age. This specialized training – characterized by the typical Swiss precision – had a decisive influence on his later development as a musician.

*In 1956* – just nineteen years old – he began his professional music career in Paris and soon started playing with famous jazz musicians such as Sidney Bechet, Albert Nicholas and Bill Coleman.

*In 1962* he went to Stuttgart, where he played for five years with the Südfunk Tanzorchester under the direction of Erwin Lehn. Gigs with the big bands of Peter Herbolzheimer, Kurt Edelhagen and Max Greger, and with the big band of the NDR followed. At that time he made numerous recordings with leading jazz musicians from swing and bebop such as Art van Damme, Roy Eldridge, Art Farmer, Buddy de Franco, Jimmy Giuffre, Dusko Goykovich, Earl Hines and Baden Powell.

*In 1979* Charly Antolini caused a sensation with his LP "Knock Out". The record was completely sold out within days after its release. The tracks on this album showcased Charly's explosively vibrant musicianship, his outstanding timing and the Swiss precision of his drumming technique. But the tracks also fascinated the listeners because of their breathtaking dynamics, „knocking out" a good many mediocre speakers at that time.

*In 1981* Benny Goodman, the "King of Swing", invited Antolini to tour with his band through Germany and Italy. The tour ended with the legendary concert in Copenhagen on 25 December 1982, which was broadcast on TV all over Europe.

*In 1996* Charly Antolini celebrated his fortieth anniversary as a professional drummer.
His companions throughout those years include: Bruce Adams, Benny Bailey, Sidney Bechet, Eugen Cicero, Wolfgang Dauner, Barbara Dennerlein, Silvia Droste, Herb Ellis, Booker Erwin, Bud Freeman, Joe Gallardo, Herb Geller, Fatty George, Jimmy Giuffre, George Gruntz, Steve Gut, Lionel Hampton, Earl Hines, Red Holloway, Peanuts Hucko, Helen Humes, Thad Jones, Oscar Klein, Brian Lemon, Albert Mangelsdorff, Butch Miles, Red Mitchell, Dick Morrissey, Danny Moss, Romano Mussolini, Sal Nistico, Nippy Noya, Nils-Henning Örsted-Pedersen, Rebecca Parris, Fritz Pauer,

Adalar Pege, Dieter Reith, Nelson Riddle Bigband, Ack van Rooyen, Wolfgang Schmid, Wolfgang Schlüter, Len Skeat, Stuff Smith, Lew Soloff, Ralph Sutton, Clark Terry, Jean ›Toots‹ Thielemans, The Tremble Kids, Jiggs Whigham, Roy Williams und viele mehr.

## Gerald Stütz

Jahrgang 1965. Schlagzeugstudium am Peter Cornelius Konservatorium/Mainz und der Musikhochschule Köln. Privatstudium bei Charly Antolini. Konzerte und Aufnahmen mit namhaften Opern- und Konzert-Orchestern. Seit 1992 Schlagzeuger im Orchester des Staatstheaters Mainz.

Adalar Pege, Dieter Reith, Nelson Riddle Bigband, Ack van Rooyen, Wolfgang Schmid, Wolfgang Schlüter, Len Skeat, Stuff Smith, Lew Soloff, Ralph Sutton, Clark Terry, Jean ›Toots‹ Thielemans, The Tremble Kids, Jiggs Whigham, Roy Williams and many more.

## Gerald Stütz

Born in 1965, he studied percussion at the Peter Cornelius Konservatorium, Mainz, and the Musikhochschule Köln. He took private lessons with Charly Antolini, performed in concerts and recorded with well-known opera and concert orchestras. He has been a percussionist with the orchestra of the Staatstheater Mainz since 1992.

# Vorwort

Jo Jones, der legendäre Drummer von Count Basie, hat vor über dreißig Jahren einmal gesagt: „There's nothing new under the sun" („Es gibt nichts neues...") – und nun doch ein weiteres Buch zum Thema Schlagzeug? Nun, ich bin allerdings der Meinung, dass sich gerade im technischen Bereich des Schlagzeugspiels einiges geändert hat! Und weil ich seit Jahren immer wieder von vielen Drummern, sowohl von Anfängern als auch von professionellen Kollegen, mit Fragen gelöchert werde, wie ich denn dies oder jenes auf dem Drumset mache, habe ich mich entschlossen, diese *Studien* zu veröffentlichen. Ich sage bewusst *Studien*, denn dieses Buch ist keine Schlagzeugschule im herkömmlichen Sinn. Es zeigt wie *ich* spiele, und wie *ich* meine technischen Figuren auf das Drumset übertrage. Durch diese Studien kann jeder Schlagzeuger lernen, genauso zu spielen wie ich, wenn er nur intensiv genug mit diesem Material arbeitet.

Da ich viel lieber spiele, als Punkte, Kreuzchen und Striche aufs Papier zu malen, bin ich sehr glücklich, dass Gerald Stütz mir mit unermüdlichem Fleiß und großer Fachkompetenz bei der Schreibarbeit zu diesem Buch zur Seite stand. Gerald ist ein hervorragender junger Drummer – und, „so ganz nebenbei", auch noch klassischer Schlagzeuger am Staatstheater Mainz. Damit ihr hören könnt, wie diese Studien klingen, habe ich die meisten auf der beiliegenden CD eingespielt. So bekommt ihr den richtigen Eindruck davon, wie ich am Drumset agiere und wie ich meine technischen Möglichkeiten einsetze.

Wir wünschen allen viel Freude und Spaß, und vor allem viel Erfolg!

Charly Antolini und Gerald Stütz

# Foreword

More than thirty years ago, Jo Jones, Count Basie's legendary drummer, said: *"There's nothing new under the sun"* – and now here is yet another book on drums! However, I think that especially the technical aspect of drumming has changed considerably, and because many drummers, both beginners and professional colleagues, kept asking me how I do this or that on the drum set, I decided to publish these *Studies*. I deliberately call them *Studies* because this is not a conventional drum methods book. It shows how *I* play and how *I* realize technical patterns on the drum set. With the help of these studies every drummer can learn to play the way I do, if they only spend enough time studying the material.

Since I prefer playing to scribbling dots, crosses and lines on a piece of paper, I am very happy that Gerald Stütz with his tireless diligence and great competence assisted me in actually writing this book. Gerald is an outstanding young drummer – and, as a "sideline" – even a classical percussionist at the Staatstheater Mainz. I have recorded most of the studies on the enclosed CD so that you can hear what they should sound like. In this way you can get the right impression of how I play the drums and how I implement my technical possibilities. We wish everyone a lot of joy and fun, especially success, too!

Charly Antolini and Gerald Stütz

# Üben – aber richtig

Beim Üben habe ich persönlich immer darauf geachtet, mich immer *nur mit einer* rhythmischen Figur oder Grundlage zu befassen – so lange, bis ich sie sicher spielen konnte.

Die Angewohnheit vieler Schlagzeuger „ein bisschen hier und ein bisschen da" zu üben ist meiner Überzeugung nach reiner Zeitverlust und bringt auf Dauer gesehen nicht viel.

Wenn man sich aber beim Üben lediglich auf eine Figur oder Grundlage konzentriert, entsteht automatisch ein natürlicher Bewegungsablauf. Ganz wichtig: Hände, Füße und Arme so locker wie möglich halten – nicht verkrampfen!

# Practising – The Proper Way

When practising, I used to take care to study *only one* rhythmic pattern or basic technique and continue practising it until I felt confident about playing it. I am convinced that the habit of many drummers of practising "a little here and a little there" is a waste of time and will amount to nothing in the long run.

By concentrating on just one pattern or basic technique, a natural sequence of movements will develop. Most importantly, make sure your hands, feet and arms are relaxed – don't be tense!

## Drum-Key

## Drum-Key

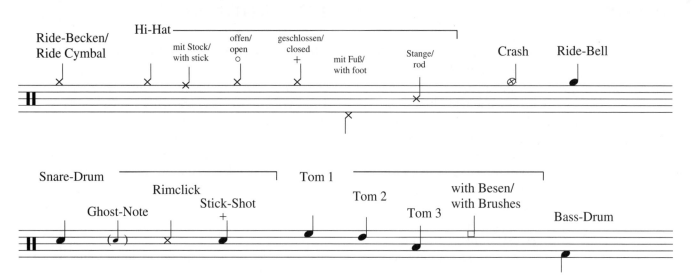

# Die Grundlagen – Schweizer Trommeln

# The Basics – Swiss Drumming

Gerne erinnere ich mich an die Zeit, als ich das Trommeln „von der Pike auf" lernen durfte. Mein Trommel-Lehrer hieß Karl Ostertag. Er stammte aus Basel, und ich fand es einfach super, dass ich von ihm auch das „Basler-Trommeln" lernen konnte. Im Frühjahr 1947, ich war noch keine 10 Jahre alt, hatte ich innerhalb von sechs Monaten bei ihm schon die wichtigsten Grundlagen gelernt. Karl Ostertag war wirklich ein sehr guter Lehrer. Er achtete besonders darauf, dass man sich eine saubere und genaue Trommeltechnik aneignete. Noch heute höre ich seine Worte: „Nicht pfuschen, und immer schön gleichmäßig üben!"

I like to reminisce about the time when I began to learn drumming "from scratch". My drum teacher was Karl Ostertag. He was born in Basel and I thought it was just great that I had the chance to learn "Basel style" drumming from him. By the spring of 1947, when I was not even 10 years old, I had learned the most important basics from him within six months. Karl Ostertag was really a very good teacher. He made sure that his students developed correct and accurate drum techniques. I can still hear him saying: "Don't be sloppy, and always practise regularly!"

10

## Schweizer Tagwacht

Dieses Stück ist eine Kombination aus 3er-, 5er-, 7er- und 9er-Rufen.

## Schweizer Tagwacht

This piece is a combination of 3-, 5-, 7- and 9-stroke rolls.

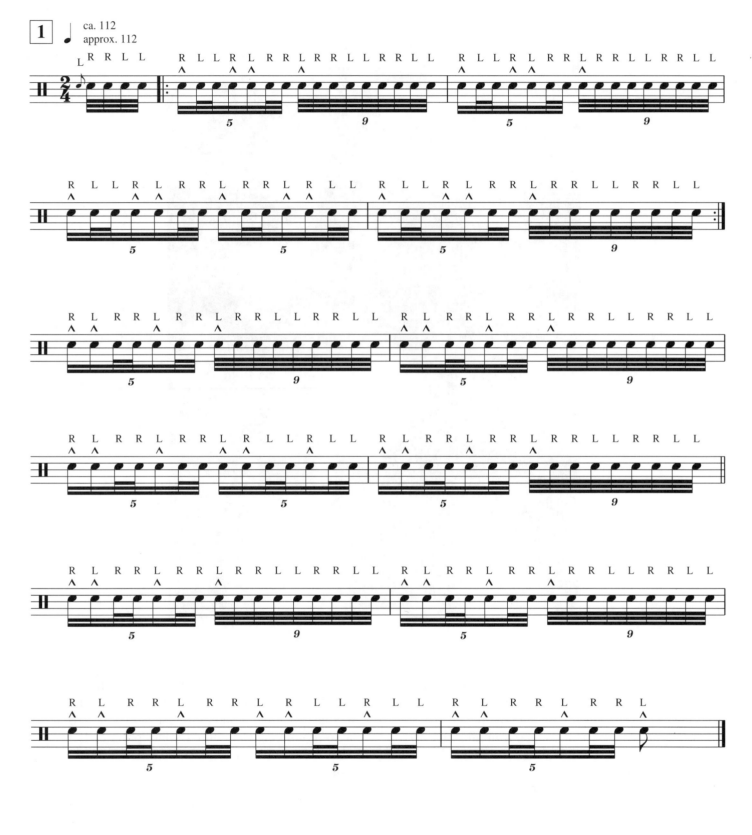

# Der Wirbel

Die wichtigste Grundlage jeder Trommeltechnik ist und bleibt der Wirbel. Gemeint ist hier der „Papa-Mama"-Wirbel, also RRLL, LLRR. Nicht zu verwechseln mit dem klassischen Orchesterwirbel.

# The Roll

The roll is still the most important element of every drum technique. I am talking about the "mama and papa" roll here, i.e. RRLL, LLRR. Don't confuse it with the classical orchestra roll.

Beim Wirbel lasse ich die Stöcke nicht springen, sondern ich schlage grundsätzlich alles aus. Das heißt: pro Hand immer jeweils zwei Schläge, wobei die zweite Note genauso „stark" angeschlagen wird wie die erste! Nur so klingt ein Wirbel wirklich exakt.

When I play a roll I don't let the sticks bounce, but execute every stroke properly. That means, always two strokes per hand, with the second note being struck as "strongly" as the first one! This is the only way to make a roll sound really accurate.

# Die Rufe

Mit Ruf bezeichnen wir die Anzahl der Trommel-schläge eines Wirbels. Ein 5er-Ruf hat also 5 Schläge, usw. Die in der Schweizer Trommeltechnik am meisten verwendeten sind die 3er-, 5er-, 7er- und 9er-Rufe. Darüber hinaus gibt es 11er-, 13er-, 15er- und 17er-Rufe.

# The Strokes

The number of drum beats of a roll are called strokes. Thus a 5-stroke roll consists of 5 strokes, etc. The rolls most commonly used in Swiss drum technique are the 3-, 5-, 7- and 9-stroke rolls.
There are also 11-, 13-, 15- and 17-stroke rolls.

# Der 5er-Ruf

# The 5-Stroke Roll

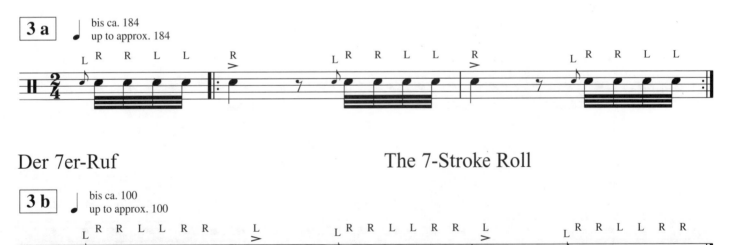

# Der 7er-Ruf

# The 7-Stroke Roll

## Der 9er-Ruf

## The 9-Stroke Roll

## Weitere wichtige Übungen mit Flams

## Further important exercises with flams

## Schweizer Ordonnanztriole

## Schweizer Ordonnanztriole

## Der Basler Trommelvorschlag
(„Schleppstreich")

## The Basel Flam
("Schleppstreich")

## Der Pata-Flafla

Eine Schweizer Trommelfigur, bei der „Pa" und „ta" für Einzelschläge, und „Fla-fla" für betonte Schläge mit Vorschlagsnoten stehen.

## The Pata-Flafla

A Swiss drum pattern, with "Pa" and "ta" indicating single strokes and "Fla-fla" indicating accented strokes with grace notes.

## Vorübung zum Pata-Flafla

## Preliminary Pata-Flafla Exercise

## Der Pata-Flafla

Langsam beginnen – schneller werden – wieder langsamer werden

## The Pata-Flafla

Start slowly – increase the tempo – slow down again

## Charly's Flam- und Paradiddle-Übungen

## Charly's Flam and Paradiddle Exercises

14

Hier zwei Beispiele die ich in der Knabenmusik Zürich im Jahr 1947 gelernt und gespielt habe.

Here are two examples which I learned and played as a boy in the "Knabenmusik Zürich" in 1947.

Und noch einige Beispiele und Übungen aus der Schweizer Trommelschule, die zur Verbesserung der Wirbeltechnik und Schnelligkeit äußerst hilfreich sind.

And some more examples and exercises from my Swiss drum school to help you improve your roll technique and speed.

## Übungen mit Triolen, 5er- und 7er-Wirbeln

Die Akzente immer stark betonen!

## Exercises with Triplets, 5- and 7-Stroke Rolls

Always fully stress the accents!

Immer zuerst langsam üben und erst nach und nach versuchen schneller zu werden.
Die Akzente betonen.

**Achtung:** In Übung 12 und 13 ist auf der „Zwei-und" eine Sextole!

Always practise slowly at first and gradually try to increase the tempo.
Stress the accents.

**Note:** There is a sextuplet on the "two and" in exercises 12 and 13!

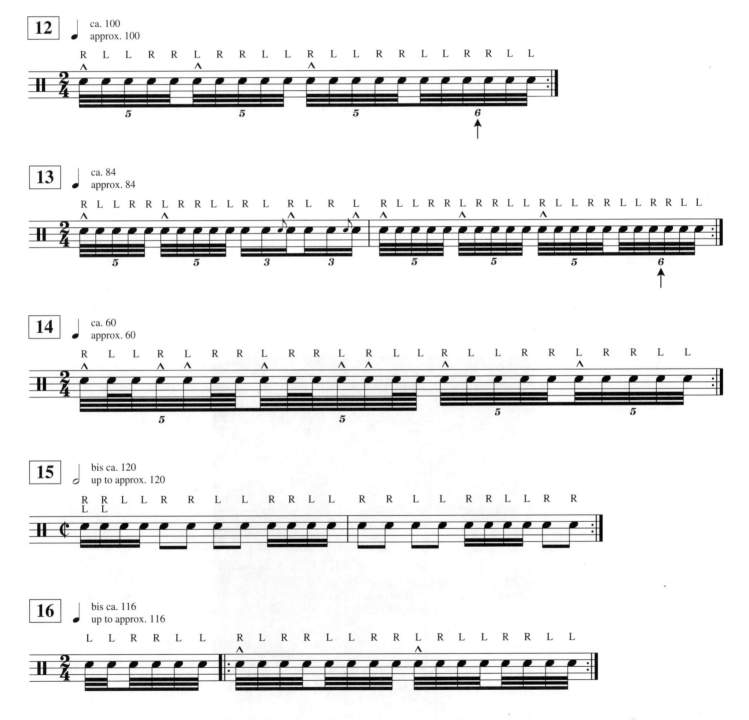

Achte bei allen Übungen zunächst nur auf die saubere Ausführung und **nicht** auf Schnelligkeit!

At first, for all exercises, focus your attention only on the accurate execution of the strokes and **not** on the tempo!

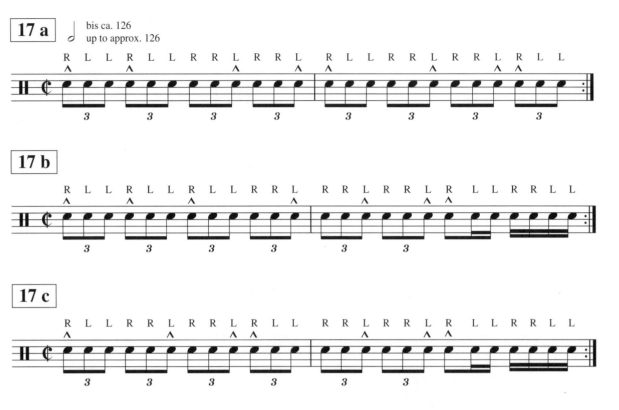

**Achtung:** Auf der „Vier" in Beispiel 18 ist eine Quintole!

**Note:** There is a quintuplet on the "four" in example 18!

# Charlys Jazz-Studien

*Keiner verkörpert für mich hierzulande den klassischen Jazz-Schlagzeugstil in der Tradition eines Jo Jones, Buddy Rich oder Mel Lewis so wie Charly Antolini. Ich finde es hervorragend, dass Charly mit diesen Studien einen Teil seiner Erfahrung und seiner lebenslangen Leidenschaft weitergibt.*
Klaus Doldinger

*Charly Antolini zählt als swingender, in der Tradition von Gene Krupa, Buddy Rich und Louie Bellson verwurzelter Schlagzeuger zur europäischen Spitzenklasse. Seine Soli zeichnen sich durch eine enorme Gestaltungskraft, Musikalität und Kreativität aus. Darüber hinaus ist Charly Antolini ein großartiger Ensemblespieler. Sein Schlagzeug ist Herz und Impulsgeber einer Band.*
Werner Stiefele (Jazz-Journalist)

# Charly's Jazz Studies

*For me, there is no greater example of classical jazz drumming in the tradition of Jo Jones, Buddy Rich or Mel Lewis, than Charly Antolini. I think it's great that Charly has decided to pass on a part of his experience and lifelong passion by publishing these studies.*
Klaus Doldinger

*Rooted in the swing tradition of Gene Krupa, Buddy Rich and Louie Bellson, Charly Antolini is one of Europe's top drummers. His solos are characterized by his tremendous inventiveness, musicianship and creativity. Furthermore, Antolini is an outstanding ensemble player. His drums are the very heart and impulse of a band.*
Werner Stiefele (jazz journalist)

Benny Goodman/Charly Antolini – 1982

18

Hier sind einige Basis-Übungen für Bass-Drum und
Hi-Hat.
Den Swing-Rhythm:

Here are some basic exercises for bass drum and hi-hat.
I always play the swing rhythm:

spiele ich dabei immer auf dem Ride-Becken mit.
Zunächst eine Übung bei der Bass-Drum und Hi-Hat
sich abwechseln:

on the ride cymbal. First, here is an exercise with alternating bass drum and hi-hat:

**19 a** ♩ bis ca. 126
up to approx. 126

Nun nehmen wir Snare-Drum- oder Toms dazu.
Mit Toms ergeben sich folgende Figuren:

Now let's add snare drum or toms. With toms you can
produce the following patterns:

**19 b**

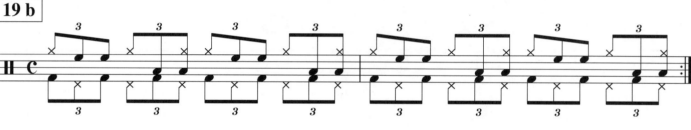

Fügen wir eine Snare-Drum-Figur in der linken Hand
dazu, etwa so:

If we add a snare drum pattern with the left hand, like
this:

ergibt sich Folgendes:

the result will be the following:

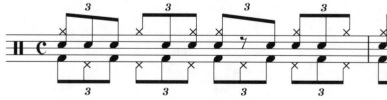

Oder nimm obige Snare-Drum-Figur und fülle die
Pausen mit der Hi-Hat aus. Das ist eine hervorragende
Übung für die Hi-Hat!

Or take the above snare drum pattern and fill the rests
with the hi-hat. This is a great hi-hat exercise!

**20 a** ♩ bis ca. 126
up to approx. 126

Hier eine Kombination mit der Bass-Drum:

Here is a combination with the bass drum:

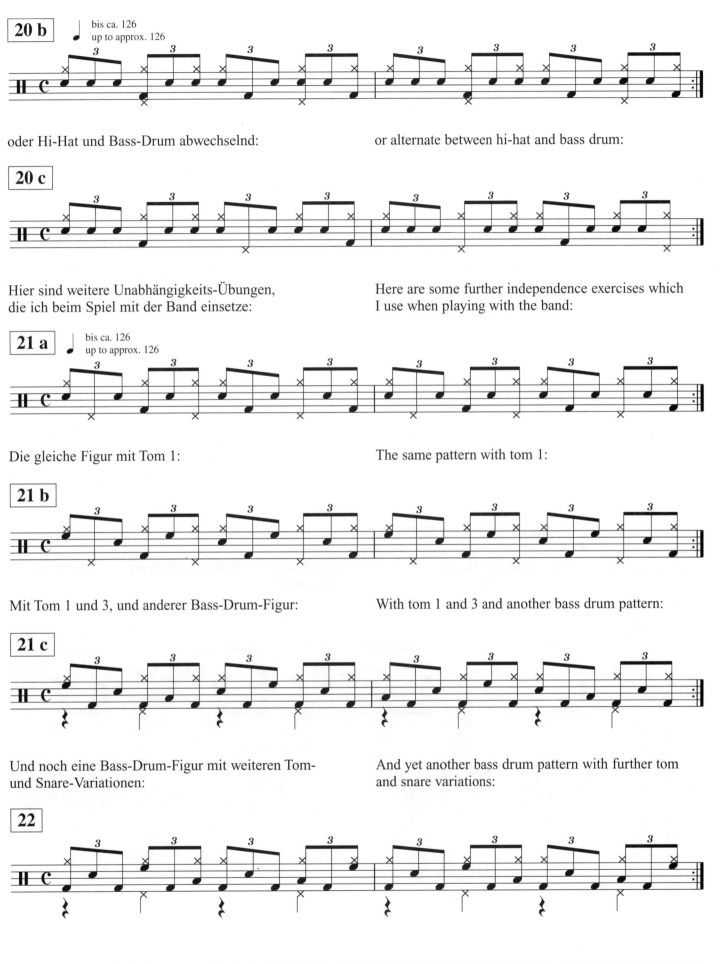

oder Hi-Hat und Bass-Drum abwechselnd:

or alternate between hi-hat and bass drum:

Hier sind weitere Unabhängigkeits-Übungen, die ich beim Spiel mit der Band einsetze:

Here are some further independence exercises which I use when playing with the band:

Die gleiche Figur mit Tom 1:

The same pattern with tom 1:

Mit Tom 1 und 3, und anderer Bass-Drum-Figur:

With tom 1 and 3 and another bass drum pattern:

Und noch eine Bass-Drum-Figur mit weiteren Tom- und Snare-Variationen:

And yet another bass drum pattern with further tom and snare variations:

Die beiden folgenden Übungen sind eine Form der „Mühle" zwischen Bass-Drum, Snare-Drum und Hi-Hat.

The following two exercises consist of double strokes alternating between bass drum, snare drum and hi-hat.

**23** ♩ ca. 132 approx. 132

Bei dieser Übung ganz besonders auf Genauigkeit achten!

Pay close attention to accuracy with this exercise!

**24** ♩ ca. 132 approx. 132

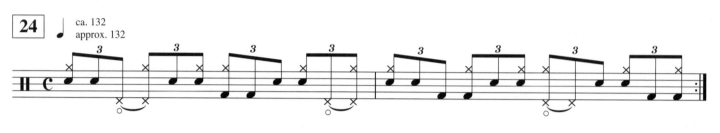

Übungen für die linke Hand:

Left-hand exercises:

**25** ♩ ca. 126 approx. 126

In Übung 26 werden Snare und Toms nur mit der linken Hand gespielt.
Wichtig: **gerade Achtel in der linken Hand!**

In exercise 26, snare and toms are played with the left hand only.
Important: **play straight eighths (quavers) with the left hand!**

**26** ♩ ca. 138 approx. 138

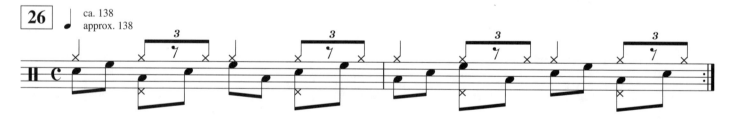

## Uptempo Swing

In sehr schnellen Tempi spielen wir die Ride-Becken-Figur fast als gerade Achtel, also so:

## Uptempo Swing

For a fast tempo, we play the ride cymbal pattern almost like straight eighths, like this:

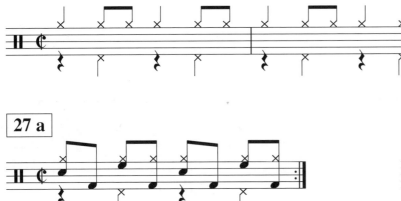

**27 a**

**27 b**

**27 c**

**27 d**

**27 e**

**27 f**

**28 a**

**28 b**

**28 c**

**28 d**

**28 e**

**28 f**

## Moderato Swing

Übung für die linke Hand

## Moderato Swing

Left-Hand Exercises

**29 a**

**29 b**

Hier nur zwei Beispiele von sehr vielen Möglichkeiten. Erfinde selbst weitere Übungen und schreibe sie auf! Dabei immer an den durchgehenden Swing-Rhythmus des Ride-Beckens denken.

Here are only two examples from many possibilities. Make up your own exercises and write them down! Keep the steady swing rhythm on the ride cymbal in mind.

Bei den folgenden Licks spiele ich Viertel-Triolen auf Snaredrum, Hi-Hat und Bassdrum. Diese Figuren klingen auch in schnellen Tempi sehr gut.

I play the following licks with quarter note triplets (crotchet triplets) on the snare drum, hi-hat and bass drum. These patterns sound very good even at fast tempos.

**30 a**

## Hi-Hat Variationen

## Hi-Hat Variations

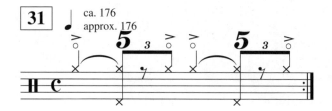

So und nicht anders muss der Hi-Hat Jazzrhythmus notiert sein, wenn er richtig klingen soll. Leider findet man aber in vielen Schlagzeug-Schulen immer noch die folgende, **falsch** klingende Notation:

To make it sound right, the hi-hat jazz rhythm must be notated like this. Unfortunately, the following **wrong** sounding notation can still be found in many drum methods:

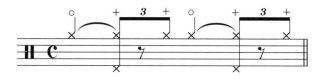

Damit die Hi-Hat Becken den richtigen Sound entwickeln dürfen sie nicht zu weit geöffnet werden, es ist sogar sehr wichtig, dass sie sich noch berühren.

To develop the right sound, the hi-hat cymbals must not be opened too much. In fact, it is very important that they still touch.

## Weitere Variationen

## Further Variations

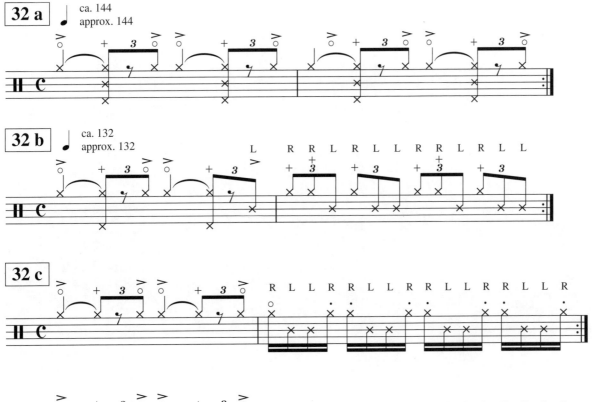

Wenn ich Bass- oder Klaviersoli begleite, schlage ich oft mit dem linken Stock noch zusätzlich gegen die Stange der Hi-Hat.

When accompanying bass or piano solos, I often also beat against the rod of the hi-hat with the left stick.

# Das Hi-Hat Glissando

Durch mehr oder weniger Druck mit dem Fuß auf das
Hi-Hat Pedal ändert sich die Tonhöhe der Hi-Hat.
Diese Technik setze ich in meinen Solos gern ein.

# The Hi-Hat Glissando

By exerting more or less pressure on the hi-hat pedal
with my foot, the pitch of the hi-hat changes. I like
using this technique in my solos.

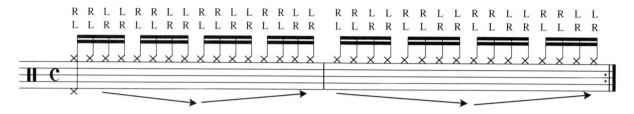

# Charlys Breaks

*Lieber Charly – „Sir Charles", für mich bist Du einer der größten Drummer dieser Welt. Deine Technik und rhythmische Geschmeidigkeit sind wunderbar. Es ist für mich eine große Ehre, dass ich schon viele Jahre dein Freund sein darf.*
Huub Janssen

# Charly's Breaks

*Dear Charly – "Sir Charles", for me you are one of the greatest drummers in the world. Your technique and rhythmic smoothness are wonderful. It is a great honour for me that you have allowed me to be your friend for so many years.*
Huub Janssen

Charly Antolini / Huub Janssen / Pete York – 1997

*Vor vielen Jahren nahm ich an einer internationalen Drumbattle teil, bei der ich nach einem Typ namens Charly Antolini spielen musste. Innerhalb von ein paar Minuten spielte er alles, was man sich auf einem Schlagzeug nur vorstellen konnte, und ich dachte: „Was zum Teufel ist denn jetzt noch für mich übrig?" Ich tat das Einzige, was ich tun konnte, und spielte mein Solo auf dem Crash-Becken. Charly ist einer der wenigen Bandleader/Drummer in der Szene, und ich weiß sehr gut, was das heißt. Man muss Talent, Selbstvertrauen, Entschlossenheit und eine starke Persönlichkeit haben. Charly spielt mit großer Hingabe nur Jazz vom Feinsten, und das in einer Zeit, da in den Medien nur das Mittelmaß zählt. Ich habe großen Respekt vor ihm und bin stolz auf unsere Freundschaft.*
Pete York

*Many years ago I took part in an international drumbattle where I had to follow some guy called Charly Antolini. In a few minutes he played just everything you could ever wish to hear on a drum set, and I was thinking: "What the hell's left for me to do?" I did the only thing I could and played my solo on the splash cymbal. Charly is one of the few bandleader/drummers on the scene and I know very well what that entails. You need talent, self-confidence, determination and a strong personality. Charly is dedicated to playing and presenting the best in jazz at a time when the media champions only the mediocre. He has my true respect and I'm proud of our friendship.*
Pete York

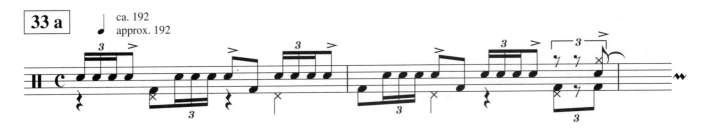

33 b ist der gleiche Break wie 33 a, aber durch Hinzunahme des Ride-Beckens anders instrumentiert.

33 b is the same break as 33 a, but scored differently because of the ride cymbal addition.

Bei den folgenden Breaks werden nur Bass-Drum und Hi-Hat variiert.

In the following breaks, only the bass drum and the hi-hat are varied.

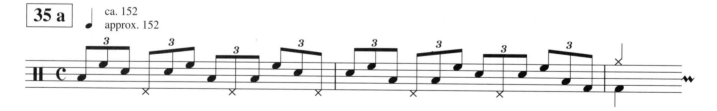

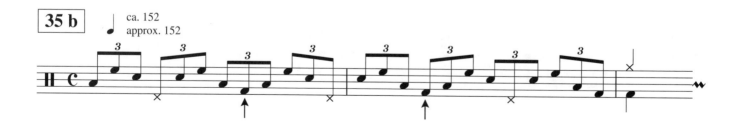

**35 c** ♩ ca. 152 / approx. 152

Bei den nächsten Breaks setze ich stellenweise die Bass-Drum als „dritte Hand" ein.

In the next breaks, I sometimes employ the bass drum as a "third hand".

**36** ♩ ca. 160 / approx. 160

**37** ♩ ca. 176 / approx. 176

**38** ♩ ca. 176 / approx. 176

**39** ♩ ca. 152 / approx. 152

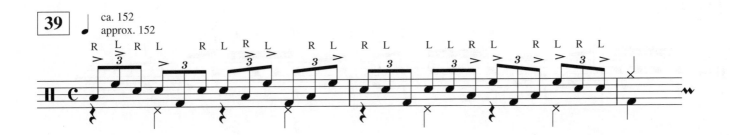

**40** ♩ ca. 208 / approx. 208

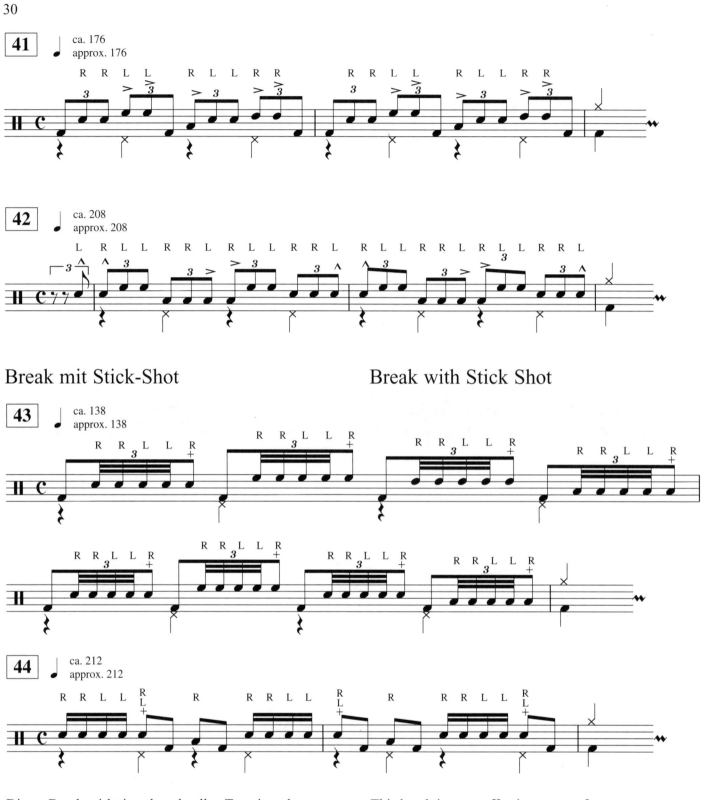

## Break mit Stick-Shot

## Break with Stick Shot

Dieser Break wirkt in sehr schnellen Tempi am besten.

This break is most effective at very fast tempos.

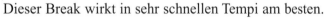

**46**  ♩ ca. 224 / approx. 224

In dieser Übung unbedingt das *crescendo* beachten!

Notice the *crescendo* in this exercise!

**47 a**  ♩ ca. 232 / approx. 232

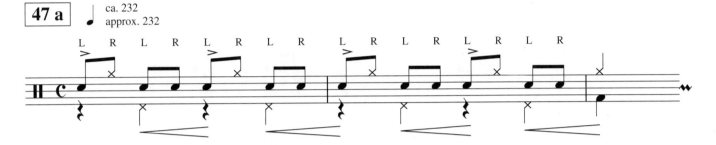

Hier kommt die gleiche Figur wie vorher, jedoch mit einem kurzen Presswirbel in der linken Hand auf die „1" und die „3".

This is the same pattern as before, but with a short press roll in the left hand on the "1" and the "3".

**47 b**

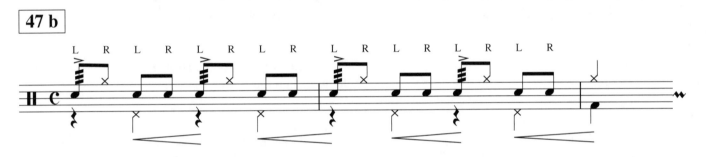

Und nun das Gleiche in Triolenform:

And now the same with triplets:

**47 c**  ♩ ca. 160 / approx. 160

**47 d**  ♩ ca. 160 / approx. 160

Hier ist ein Solo-Break mit Schweizer Trommeltechnik. In sehr schnellem Tempo sind nur die Akzente und ein scheinbar durchgehender Wirbel auf der Snare-Drum zu hören.

Here is a solo break using the Swiss drum technique. When played very fast, you can only hear the accents and a seemingly continuous roll on the snare drum.

Dies ist die sogenannte „Mühle" in Triolenform. Sie dient als Vorübung zu dem folgenden zweitaktigen Solo.

These are double strokes with triplets. They serve as a preliminary exercise for the following two-bar solo.

Achte besonders auf die Doppelschläge zwischen den Toms und der Snare.

Concentrate on the double strokes alternating between the toms and the snare.

In dieser Übung sollte die Snare sehr leise gespielt werden, damit die Akzente der Toms deutlich zur Geltung kommen.

In this exercise the snare should be played very softly, so that the accents of the toms can be clearly heard.

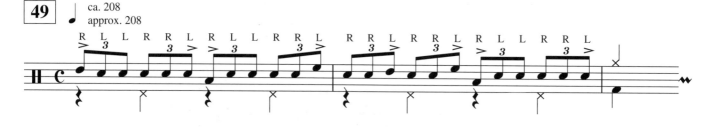

Ein Break mit Crash-Becken auf der linken und rechten Seite.

A break with crash cymbals on the left and on the right.

Hier sind drei Vorübungen für den nachfolgenden Break:

Here are three preliminary exercises for the following break:

Hier ist ein schöner Break mit Stick-Shot und einem „Drei über Vier"-Feeling.

Here is a nice break with a stick shot and a "three over four" feel.

Dieser Break mit Quintolen – aufgeteilt zwischen Toms, Snare und Bass-Drum ist besonders in schnellem Tempo sehr wirkungsvoll.

This break with quintuplets – distributed between toms, snare and bass drum, is particularly effective when played at a fast tempo.

Ein einfacher Paradiddle mit geraden Achtelnoten als Break:

A simple paradiddle with straight eighths in the form of a break:

34

Hier zeige ich dir einige Triolenfiguren im Blues-Shuffle-Tempo:

Now let me show you some triplet patterns at a blues-shuffle tempo:

# Der zweifache Paradiddle

# The Double Paradiddle

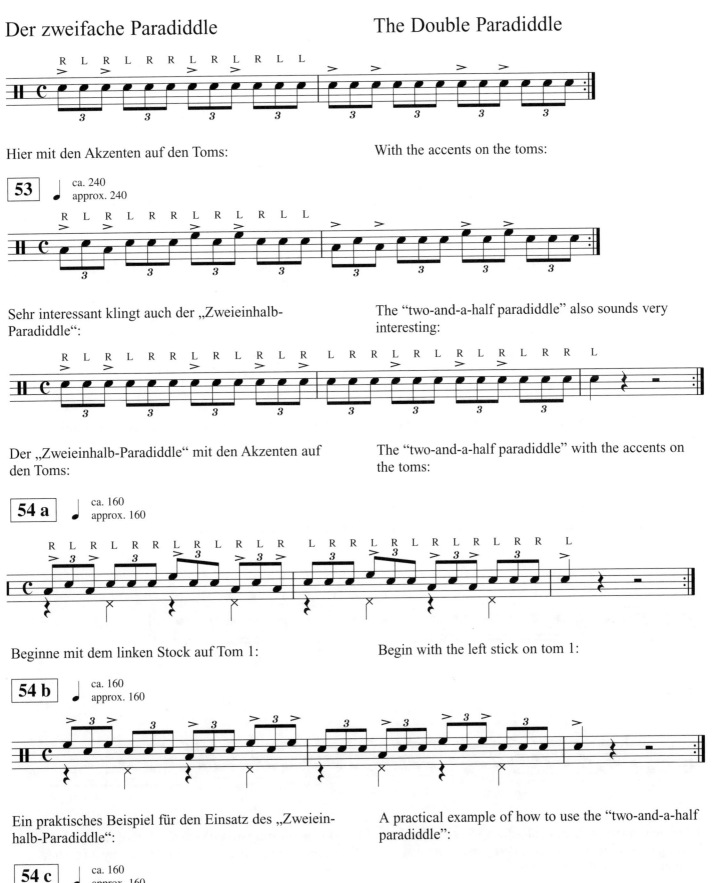

Hier mit den Akzenten auf den Toms:

With the accents on the toms:

Sehr interessant klingt auch der „Zweieinhalb-Paradiddle":

The "two-and-a-half paradiddle" also sounds very interesting:

Der „Zweieinhalb-Paradiddle" mit den Akzenten auf den Toms:

The "two-and-a-half paradiddle" with the accents on the toms:

Beginne mit dem linken Stock auf Tom 1:

Begin with the left stick on tom 1:

Ein praktisches Beispiel für den Einsatz des „Zweiein-halb-Paradiddle":

A practical example of how to use the "two-and-a-half paradiddle":

**55 a** ♩ ca. 160 / approx. 160

Noch einmal der gleiche Break, aber diesmal mit links beginnend.

The same break again, but this time beginning with the left hand.

Nun zunächst zwei Vorübungen zu den nachfolgenden Soli:

Here are two preliminary exercises for the following solos:

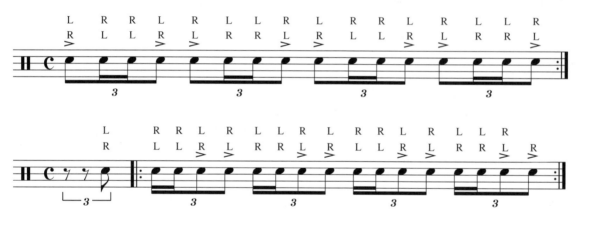

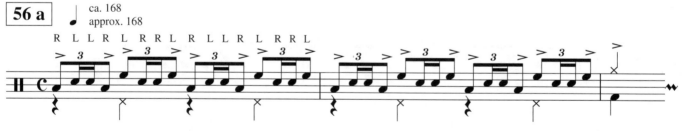

**56 a** ♩ ca. 168 / approx. 168

Es ist sehr interessant zu beobachten wie sich das Feeling dieses kleinen Solos ändert, wenn man den Anfang um ein Achtel nach vorne verschiebt.

It is interesting to see how the feel of this little solo changes by moving the beginning up by an eighth.

**56 b** ♩ ca. 168 / approx. 168

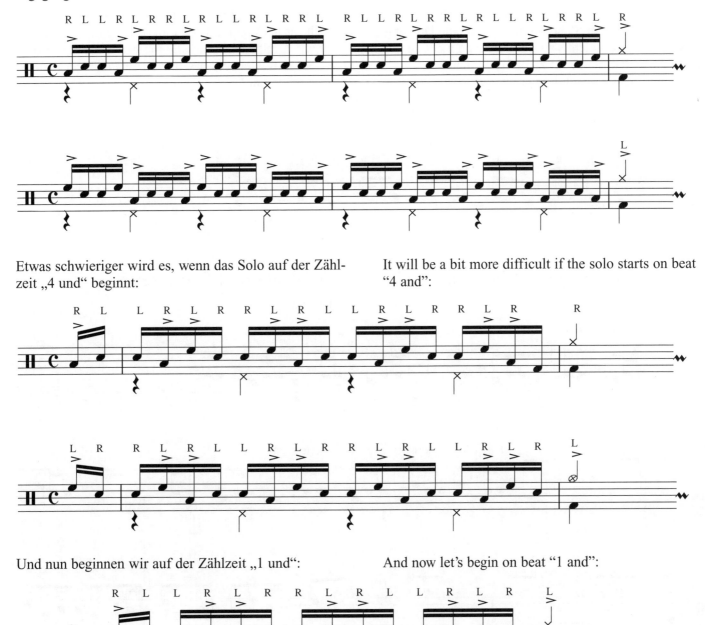

Beachte nun den rhythmischen Unterschied zu den vorangegangenen Soli!

Now notice the rhythmic difference from the previous solos!

Etwas schwieriger wird es, wenn das Solo auf der Zählzeit „4 und" beginnt:

It will be a bit more difficult if the solo starts on beat "4 and":

Und nun beginnen wir auf der Zählzeit „1 und":

And now let's begin on beat "1 and":

Bei einem Solo ist unbedingt wichtig immer genau zu wissen auf welcher Zählzeit man gerade ist. Eine gute Hilfe ist es, wenn man beim Üben innerlich eine Melodie „mitsingt", z. B. „Sweet Georgia Brown" (Thema: 2 mal 16 Takte). Mit diesem einfachen Hilfsmittel lässt sich ein Drumsolo musikalisch interessant gestalten.

Bei diesem Solo-Break kommt es darauf an die betonten Schläge auf dem Standtom nur durch eine Drehung des rechten Handgelenks auszuführen und nicht den ganzen Arm zum Standtom zu bewegen. Unnötige Bewegungsabläufe gehen immer nur auf Kosten der Geschwindigkeit!

When playing solo, it is essential that you always know exactly which part of the bar you are on. It's helpful to hum along silently, e.g. a melody such as "Sweet Georgia Brown" (theme: 2 times 16 bars). You can make a drum solo very interesting with the aid of this simple method.

The most important thing in this solo break is to execute the strokes on the floor tom by only turning the right wrist, rather than moving the whole arm toward the floor tom. Unnecessary movements only serve to reduce the tempo!

**57** ♩ ca. 232
approx. 232

## Zusammenfassung der Übungen 56 a und 56 b:

## Combination of Exercises 56 a and 56 b:

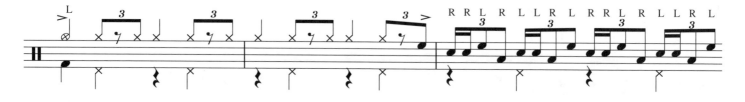

40

Bei der folgenden Übung die Akzente auf den Toms deutlich hervorheben.

Fully stress the accents on the toms in the following exercise.

Eine gute Einspiel-Übung für das Drumset:

A good warm-up exercise for the drum set:

Ein typischer Bigband-Break:

A typical big band break:

Zunächst die Grundfigur für die nachfolgenden Breaks:

First, the basic pattern for the following breaks:

Variation:

Variation:

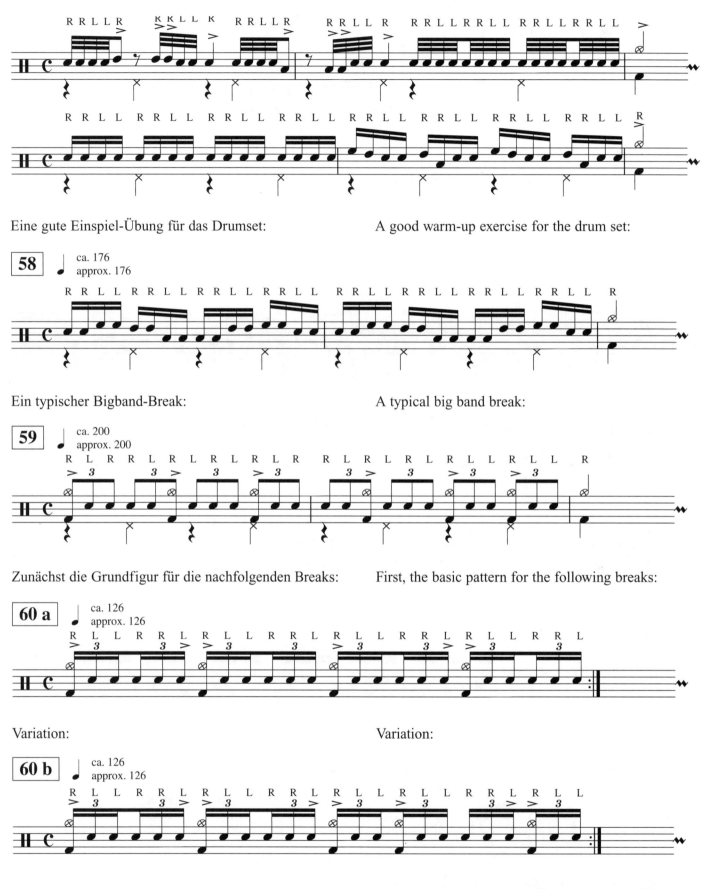

**60 c** ♩ ca. 232
approx. 232

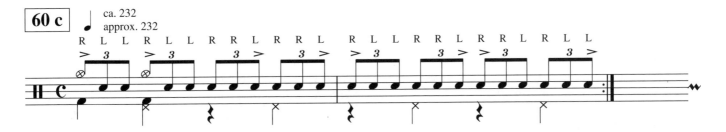

Die folgende Solofigur hat es in sich! Achte genau auf den Handsatz.

This is quite a solo pattern! Concentrate on your hand setting.

**61** ♩ bis ca. 168
up to approx. 168

42

# Charlys Latin Corner

*Charly Antolini – ein Schlagzeuger der absoluten Spitzenklasse. Durch seine Perfektion, Technik und Ausdauer hat er acht Jahre meine Bigband bereichert. Seine Drumsoli sind meiner Meinung nach in Europa einmalig. Für jeden Drummer kann er eigentlich nur Vorbild sein.*
Max Greger

# Charly's Latin Corner

*Charly Antolini – an absolutely first-rate drummer. For eight years, my big band was enhanced by his perfection, technique and endurance. In my opinion, his drum solos are unique in Europe. He is a great example for every drummer.*
Max Greger

*Charly Antolini achte ich als Meilenstein in der internationalen Drummer-Szene. Er hat ganze Generationen von Schlagzeugern beeinflusst und jeder junge Drummer ist gut beraten, sich ausgiebig mit Charlys Spielweise zu befassen.*
Joachim Fuchs-Charrier

*I respect Charly Antolini as a milestone on the international drummer scene. He has influenced whole generations of drummers, and I advise every young drummer to thoroughly study Charly's playing technique.*
Joachim Fuchs-Charrier

Die folgenden Beispiele stellen immer nur die Basispattern dar. Beim Spielen dürfen und sollen die Rhythmen immer leicht abgewandelt werden.

The following examples only consist of the basic patterns. When playing, you may and should always slightly vary the rhythms.

## Afro-Cuban

## Afro-Cuban

## Latin Funk

## Latin Funk

## Mambo

## Mambo

**63** ♩ ca. 92
approx. 92

## Bossa

## Bossa

**64** ♩ ca. 92
approx. 92

Bei schnellen Tempi ist der folgende Rhythmus besonders effektvoll:

The following rhythm is particularly effective at fast tempos:

**65** ♩ ca. 100
approx. 100

Und hier sind einige meiner Latin-Grooves:

And here are some of my Latin grooves:

**66 a** ♩ ca. 100
approx. 100

44

Bei der folgenden Samba-Figur spielt die linke Hand mit Besen, die rechte mit Stock. Der Besen bleibt dabei, quasi als Dämpfung, mit seiner ganzen Fläche auf dem Tom liegen.

Play the following samba pattern with the brush in the left and the stick in the right hand. The whole brush should remain on the tom to produce a dampening effect.

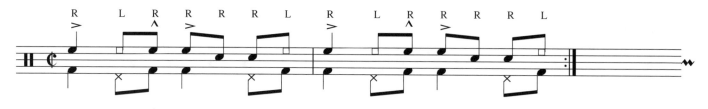

Bei den nächsten Übungen kommt es darauf an, mit der rechten Hand eine immer gleich bleibende Figur zu spielen (hier die Beckenglocke), während die linke Hand frei improvisieren kann.

For the following exercises, you need to play a consistent pattern with the right hand (in this case, the ride bell) while allowing your left hand to freely improvise.

Beispiel für die linke Hand:

Example for the left hand:

Zusammen gespielt ergibt das:

By combining them you get:

Interessante Kombinationen entstehen auch, wenn wir Ride-Becken und Hi-Hat mit der linken Hand spielen. Dazu muss ein Ride-Becken natürlich auf der linken Seite stehen.

Playing the ride cymbal and hi-hat with the left hand will also create interesting combinations. For this purpose, of course, the ride cymbal must be placed to your left.

Die Hi-Hat öffnet sich automatisch, wenn wir sie auf die Zählzeiten „1" und „3" mit dem Fuß schließen.

The hi-hat will open automatically if you close it with your foot on beats "1" and "3".

Noch einige weitere Beispiele für die linke, bzw. rechte Hand:

Further examples for the left and right hand:

# Funky Time

# Funky Time

*Mein Freund Charly Antolini ist für mich der große Bigband- und Jazzdrummer, den ich schon als Kind im Fernsehen bewundert habe. Da war dieser Kerl am Schlagzeug, der über der ganzen Bigband thronte und mehr Dominanz ausstrahlte als alle zusammen. Charly Antolini, das ist für mich:*
- immer *ein super Feeling zu seinen Mitmusikern, trotz unbändiger Power.*
- immer *konzentriert und engagiert, trotzdem wild und mutig.*
- immer *offene Ohren und Interesse für neue Ideen und Einflüsse, und vor allem:*
- immer *Charly geblieben.*

Curt Cress

*For me, my friend Charly Antolini is still the great big band and jazz drummer I used to admire on TV when I was a child. There was this guy on the drum set, overlooking the whole big band and exuding more dominance than all of the others put together: Charly Antolini, to me that means*
- always *maintaining a superb awareness of his fellow musicians, despite his enormous power.*
- always *concentrated and committed, although wild und courageous.*
- always *open to and interested in new ideas and influences, and, above all:*
- always *remaining true to himself.*

Curt Cress

Beim Üben hat sich die folgende Vorgehensweise als praktisch und effektiv erwiesen: Ich nehme zunächst eine Hi-Hat Grundfigur, zum Beispiel:

The following practising routine has proved to be practical and effective. First, I take a basic hi-hat pattern, for example:

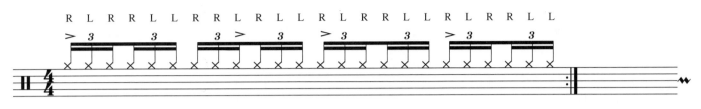

Nun überlege ich mir dazu passende Bass- und Snaredrum Akzente:

Then I add some bass and snare drum accents that go with it:

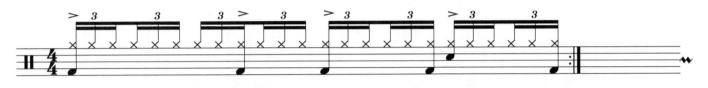

Nun variiere ich die Akzente der Bassdrum:

Then I vary the bass drum accents:

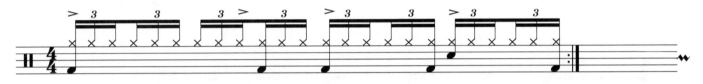

und eine weitere Akzent-Figur für die Bassdrum:

and another accent pattern for the bass drum:

Dies ist die Intro zu dem Titel „Flip Chart" von der LP „Menue":

This is the intro to the title "Flip Chart" from the LP "Menue":

Der Groove des Titels „Co-Pilot" von der LP „Crash":

The groove of the title "Co-Pilot" from the LP "Crash":

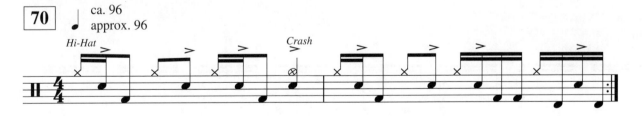

48

Weitere Funk-Grooves:

More funk grooves:

**71** ♩ ca. 96
approx. 96

Bei obigem Rhythmus spielen die rechte Hand und der linke Fuß folgende durchgehende Figur:

For the above rhythm, your right hand and left foot play the following continuous pattern:

Vorübung zum folgenden Funk-Beat:

Preliminary exercise for the following funk beat:

**72** ♩ ca. 96
approx. 96

Hi-Hat-Figur zum folgenden Funk-Beat:                    Hi-hat pattern for the following funk beat:

# Two (Breaks) For You

*Ich habe selten einen Drummer erlebt, der so viel Drive und ein solch hervorragendes Timing hat, wie Charly Antolini. Aber seine besondere Stärke liegt in seiner Vielseitigkeit. Er ist ein ausgezeichneter Solist mit einer enormen Technik und ein ebenso einfühlsamer Begleiter. Für mich ist es immer eine Freude, mit Charly einen Jazzabend auf der Bühne zu verbringen.*
Dusko Gojkovic

*In all den Jahren als Bandleader der RIAS Bigband Berlin, sowie als Pianist konnte ich mir keinen besseren Drummer wünschen als Charly Antolini. Charly wird von allen Musikern als großartiger Techniker geschätzt, aber auch als sensibler, musikalischer und powervoll swingender Drummer. Alles Gute Charly!*
*Dein Freund* Horst Jankowski

# Two (Breaks) For You

*I have rarely heard a drummer with so much power and such a superb sense of timing like Charly Antolini. But his main strength lies in his versatility. He is an outstanding soloist with a magnificent technique as well as a highly sensitive accompanist. It is always a pleasure to spend a jazz evening on stage with Charly.*
Dusko Gojkovic

*In all those years as band leader of the RIAS Bigband, Berlin, and as a pianist, I couldn't have wished for a better drummer than Charly Antolini. All musicians respect Charly as a great artisan, but also as a sensitive, musical and powerfully swinging drummer. All the best, Charly!*
*Your friend,* Horst Jankowski

# Two (Breaks) For You
Gerald Stütz

Diese Breaks zuerst langsam beginnen, dann das Tempo steigern und wieder langsamer werden.

# Two (Breaks) For You
Gerald Stütz

Start these breaks off slowly, then increase the tempo, and slow down again.

# Daddy's Funk

# Daddy's Funk

# Samba para Renata

# Samba para Renata

Zum Einüben schwieriger Rhythmen ist es hilfreich, die rhythmische Figur in ihre Einzelteile zu zerlegen. Am Beispiel von „Samba para Renata" kann das in etwa so aussehen: Zuerst sehen wir uns an, was die Füße zu spielen haben:

When practising more difficult rhythms, it is useful to break the rhythmic pattern into its individual parts. Taking "Samba para Renata" as an example, it could look like this: first, let's have a look at what the feet need to play:

Die Hi-Hat spielt hier also eine sogenannte „3-2 Clave", während die Bassdrum das „Samba-Pattern" spielt.

The hi-hat is playing a so-called "3-2 clave" while the bass drum is playing the "samba pattern".

Die folgenden Übungen A bis F trainieren die Unabhängigkeit der Füße.

The following exercises A to F are independence exercises for the feet.

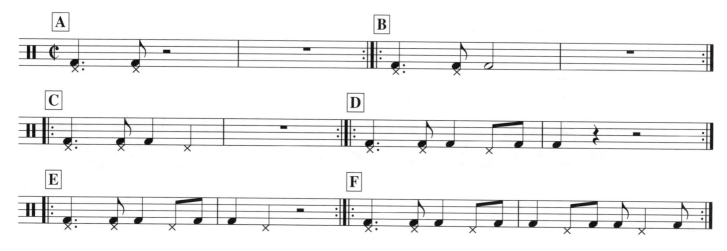

Es kommt darauf an jede Übung so oft zu wiederholen, bis sich ein Gefühl für den Groove einstellt. Es ist ausschlaggebend für Erfolg oder Misserfolg erst dann zur nächsten Übung weiterzugehen, wenn die vorhergehende *in jedem Tempo* beherrscht wird!
Hier sind nun die Figuren der Bassdrum und der Hi-Hat zur Samba.

It is essential to repeat each exercise until you get a feeling for the groove. You determine success or failure by only moving on to the next exercise after having mastered the previous one *at any tempo!*
Now, here is what bass drum and hi-hat are playing in our samba pattern:

Du solltest dieses Pattern täglich mehrmals fünf Minuten *ohne Unterbrechung* üben, damit es dir richtig vertraut wird.

You should practise this pattern several times a day for about five minutes *without a break*, so you can get really familiar with it.

Zunächst also zur „Hand-Arbeit"!
Die rechte Hand spielt immer folgendes Ostinato:

So, first of all, let's do the "manual work"!
The right hand always plays the following ostinato:

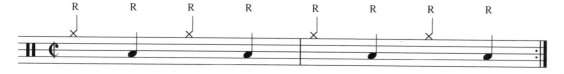

Die linke Hand setzt diesem Ostinato eine Samba-Figur auf der Snaredrum entgegen:

The left hand contrasts the ostinato by adding a samba pattern on the snare drum:

| Beide Figuren zusammen sehen so aus: | A combination of both patterns looks like this: |

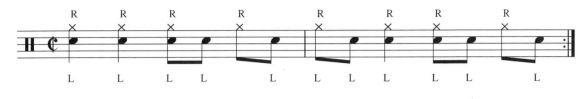

Übertrage diese Figur erst dann, wenn du sie ganz sicher beherrschst! Beginne danach erst *langsam* und übe den ganzen Rhythmus ein.

Don't employ this pattern until you feel really confident using it! After that, start *slowly* and practise the whole rhythm.

**78 a+b**  ♩ ca. 88-126  
approx. 88-126

Und nun:

*Mach weiter – viel Spaß – und lass es grooven!*

And now:

*Ride on – have fun – and keep on groovin'!*

54

# CD-Index

| Track | Titel |
|-------|-------|
| 1 | „Schweizer Tagwacht" |
| 2–18 | Grundlagen/Schweizer Trommeln |
| 19–32 | Charlys Jazz-Studien |
| 33–61 | Charlys Breaks |
| 62–68 | Charlys Latin Corner |
| 69–74 | Funky Time |
| 75–78 | Two (Breaks) For You – mit Gerald Stütz am Drumset |

**24**

Diese Kennzeichnung bei einem Notenbeispiel bedeutet: Das Beispiel ist auf Track 24 der beiliegenden CD zu hören.

Aufgenommen im Traumraum-Tonstudio, Augsburg, Toningenieur: Hartmut Welz
Gemischt bei „Straight up Productions",
Hartmut Welz/Burgau
CD-Mastering: Tonbox/Bad Überkingen

# CD-Index

| Track | Title |
|-------|-------|
| 1 | "Schweizer Tagwacht" |
| 2–18 | Basics/Swiss Drumming |
| 19–32 | Charly's Jazz Studies |
| 33–61 | Charly's Breaks |
| 62–68 | Charly's Latin Corner |
| 69–74 | Funky Time |
| 75–78 | Two (Breaks) For You – with Gerald Stütz on Drums |

**24**

An example marked in this manner denotes that you can listen to it on track 24 of the enclosed CD.

Recorded at Traumraum-Tonstudio, Augsburg, Sound Engineer: Hartmut Welz
Mixed at "Straight up Productions",
Hartmut Welz/Burgau
CD-Mastering: Tonbox/Bad Überkingen

Translation: Heike Brühl

PETER GIGER

# DIE KUNST DES RHYTHMUS

**Professionelles Know How
in Theorie und Praxis**

*Mit einem Beitrag
von Michael Küttner*

SCHOTT

Bestell-Nr. ED 7868                    ISBN 3-7957-1862-7